# The Starry Guide to Herbal Harmony

# The Starry Guide to Herbal Harmony

## VOLUME 1

Matthew Petchinsky

Apophis Enterprises LLC

# 1

∾

<u>The Starry Guide to Herbal Harmony:</u>
<u>Volume 1</u>
By:Matthew Petchinsky

**Introduction: Rekindling the Celestial Connection**

Welcome to "The Starry Guide to Herbal Harmony: Volume 1," a unique exploration into the ancient and mystical practice of Astro-Herbology. This guide is an invitation to journey through the celestial highways that connect the cosmos to the roots of our earthly existence. AstroHerbology, the art of integrating the movements and influences of celestial bodies with herbal medicine, is not merely a field of study—it is a way of reconnecting with the harmonious dance of the universe.

**The Ancient Roots of AstroHerbology**

Our journey begins by delving deep into the ancient roots of Astro-Herbology. This practice is not a new-age phenomenon but is steeped in the traditions and wisdom of several ancient civilizations, including the Egyptians, Greeks, Chinese, and Indians. Each of these cultures observed the skies and noted the intricate patterns of the stars and planets. They believed that these celestial bodies held profound influence over the natural world, including the plants that have been used for healing for millennia.

AstroHerbology marries astrology, the study of the stars and their influence on human affairs, with herbalism, the traditional medicinal practice of using plants and their extracts. Ancient astrologers and herbalists noted that certain plants responded to the energies of specific planets and zodiac signs. For example, the fiery nature of Mars could be seen in the thorny and invigorating rosemary, a herb believed to bolster both the body and spirit.

By tracing the historical tapestry of these intertwined disciplines from their origins to modern-day practices, this section aims to illuminate the depth and complexity of this celestial tradition. This historical journey not only reveals the evolution of AstroHerbology but also demonstrates its relevance and resurgence in our contemporary quest for holistic and integrative wellness approaches.

**Understanding the Cosmos and Its Influence on Plants**

The cosmos is a vast and dynamic expanse in which the celestial bodies—particularly the planets and the moon—play a significant role in influencing life on Earth. In this section, we explore how these celestial forces exert their effects on plant life, impacting everything from growth cycles to medicinal properties. The moon's gravitational pull, for instance, affects the moisture in the soil, influencing seed germination and plant growth phases. Planetary alignments and zodiacal positions are also considered to impact the potency of herbs when harvested at specific times.

This overview serves as both a scientific and mystical explanation of these phenomena, offering insights into how ancient wisdom and modern research converge. By understanding these celestial influences, practitioners of AstroHerbology can enhance their use of herbal remedies, aligning their natural properties with the healing energies of the universe.

**How to Use This Guide**

"The Starry Guide to Herbal Harmony" is structured to not only inform but also empower. This section provides readers with practical tips on how to navigate the book effectively. Whether you are a novice seeking to understand the basics of AstroHerbology or an experienced practitioner aiming to deepen your knowledge, this guide is designed to cater to a variety of needs and interests.

Readers will learn how to tailor the information within to their personal wellness journeys and integrate AstroHerbology into daily routines. Tips on timing herbal preparations with celestial events, creating personalized herbal remedies based on one's astrological sign, and incorporating these practices into a holistic lifestyle are included. This guide aims to make AstroHerbology accessible, engaging, and a transformative part of your health and wellness regimen.

As you turn these pages, let "The Starry Guide to Herbal Harmony" rekindle your celestial connection, guiding you through a harmonious symphony of stars and botanicals. Welcome to a journey of rediscovery where the ancient wisdom of the skies enlightens modern paths to wellness.

## Chapter 1: Fundamentals of AstroHerbology

Welcome to the foundational journey into the entwining paths of astrology and herbalism, where the celestial influences meet the earthly gifts of nature. In this chapter of "The Starry Guide to Herbal Harmony: Volume 1," we will explore the essential concepts needed to grasp the intricate relationship between the stars above and the herbs below. This dual introduction serves as a guiding light for herbalists new to astrology and astrologers venturing into the realm of herbalism.

### Astrological Basics for Herbalists

Astrology is the study of the movements and relative positions of celestial bodies interpreted as having an influence on human affairs and the natural world. Here are the core elements of astrology that every herbalist should know:

1. **Zodiac Signs**: The zodiac is divided into twelve signs, each covering 30 degrees of celestial longitude, associated with a set of dates within a year. These signs—Aries, Taurus, Gemini, Cancer, Leo, Virgo, Libra, Scorpio, Sagittarius, Capricorn, Aquarius, and Pisces —are believed to influence personality traits and tendencies. Understanding these signs helps in identifying which herbs resonate best with each sign's energy.

2. **Planets**: In astrology, each planet (including the Sun and Moon, referred to as luminaries) exerts a particular influence. For instance, Mars governs energy and aggression, while Venus concerns love and beauty. Each planet also rules one or more zodiac signs and affects various bodily systems and functions, which is crucial for selecting the right herbs for health issues related to specific planetary influences.

3. **Houses**: The astrological chart is divided into twelve houses, each representing a sphere of life, such as identity, finances, communication, and relationships. The planets' positions in these houses at your birth or at the time of an event affect how their energies manifest in your life.

4. **Aspects**: Aspects are the angles planets make with each other on the zodiac wheel, influencing how the energies of the different planets combine. Major aspects include conjunctions, oppositions, trines, and squares, each bringing different challenges and harmonies.

## Herbal Basics for Astrologers

Herbalism is the practice of using plants for medicinal purposes, which involves understanding their properties, parts used, and preparation methods. Here's a primer for astrologers:

1. **Plant Identification**: Learning to correctly identify plants is foundational in herbalism. This includes recognizing plant families, species, and understanding the environments where they thrive.
2. **Medicinal Properties**: Each herb has specific medicinal properties, such as anti-inflammatory, diuretic, or antiseptic effects. These properties can be influenced by the planets and zodiac signs, aligning with the astrological aspects of a person's health needs.
3. **Methods of Preparation**: Herbs can be prepared in various ways, including teas, tinctures, capsules, and salves. The method of preparation can affect the potency and absorption of the herb's medicinal qualities.

## The Zodiac and Herbal Correspondences

Each zodiac sign has unique characteristics that correlate with specific medicinal plants. Understanding these correspondences can enhance both physical and emotional well-being. Here we detail the herbal correspondences for each zodiac sign:

- **Aries**: Herbs like nettles and basil, which stimulate the circulatory system and boost energy, resonate with Aries' fiery and dynamic nature.
- **Taurus**: Soothing and stabilizing herbs like roses and violets are beneficial for Taurus, grounding their sometimes stubborn energy.

- **Gemini**: Airy herbs such as lavender and mullein support Gemini's respiratory system and aid their communicative abilities.
- **Cancer**: Moistening herbs like cucumber and aloe vera nurture Cancer's emotional and digestive health.
- **Leo**: Heart-supporting herbs like hawthorn and sunflower echo Leo's vibrant and loving essence.
- **Virgo**: Digestive aids like dandelion and peppermint benefit Virgo, helping to streamline their meticulous energy.
- **Libra**: Herbs that support kidney balance and skin health, such as kidney beans and jasmine, harmonize with Libra's aesthetic and relational focus.
- **Scorpio**: Deep, detoxifying herbs like garlic and basil match Scorpio's intense and transformative energy.
- **Sagittarius**: Liver-supporting herbs like milk thistle and sage align with Sagittarius's expansive nature.
- **Capricorn**: Bone-strengthening herbs like comfrey and horsetail resonate with Capricorn's structured and enduring qualities.
- **Aquarius**: Nervous system supporters like lemon balm and elderflower cater to Aquarius's innovative and electrical energy.
- **Pisces**: Calming and sleep-inducing herbs like chamomile and hops soothe Pisces's empathetic and dreamy nature.

This chapter provides a comprehensive foundation for intertwining astrological knowledge with herbal practices, enhancing both understanding and application in the pursuit of health and harmony. As we continue through this guide, remember that each plant and celestial body holds the potential to significantly enhance our connection to the universe and ourselves.

Check out my Virtual dispensary for all your hemp needs: https://shift.store/sg1fan23477/retail

## Chapter 2: The Solar System's Herbal Cabinet

In "The Starry Guide to Herbal Harmony: Volume 1," we continue our exploration of AstroHerbology by delving into the celestial influences of the planets on herbal medicine. Each celestial body in our solar system imparts unique energies that resonate with specific herbs, enhancing their healing properties. This chapter elucidates how these planetary influences shape the herbal remedies used to balance our physical, emotional, and spiritual well-being.

### Sun-Influenced Herbs

The Sun, the center of our solar system, symbolizes vitality, ego, and self-expression. Herbs influenced by the Sun possess qualities that boost energy, promote a sense of self, and enhance overall vitality. These herbs are often characterized by their warm, invigorating properties and are used to strengthen the heart, improve circulation, and lift the spirits.

- **Calendula**: Radiating sunny energy, calendula is excellent for skin health, promoting healing and rejuvenation. It reflects the Sun's ability to restore and enhance vitality.
- **St. John's Wort**: Known for its antidepressant properties, this herb aligns with the Sun's light, countering darkness and depression, and boosting confidence and mood.
- **Sunflower**: Symbolically and medicinally aligned with the Sun, sunflower seeds are used for their nutritional value, supporting energy and overall health.

### Moon-Influenced Herbs

The Moon governs our emotional body, intuition, and aspects of women's health. Moon-influenced herbs often have a soothing, calming effect and are used to enhance emotional healing, promote sleep, and support reproductive health.

- **Chamomile**: With its calming effects, chamomile helps soothe emotional stress and aids in sleep, mirroring the comforting embrace of the Moon.

- **Moonwort**: True to its name, moonwort is used in traditional remedies for regulating menstrual cycles and balancing hormonal fluctuations.
- **Water Lily**: This plant's association with water, a Moon element, makes it perfect for calming the nerves and enhancing meditative states.

### Mercury-Influenced Herbs

Mercury rules communication, intellect, and travel. Herbs under Mercury's influence aid in clarity of thought, enhance communication skills, and support the respiratory and nervous systems.

- **Lavender**: Known for its calming yet mentally stimulating properties, lavender aids in clear communication and peaceful thoughts.
- **Eucalyptus**: Often used to clear airways, eucalyptus supports respiratory health, enhancing the flow of air and ideas.

### Venus-Influenced Herbs

Venus governs love, beauty, and harmony. Herbs associated with Venus often have beautifying effects, promote kidney and reproductive health, and enhance emotional balance.

- **Rose**: The quintessential herb of love, roses are used for their heart-opening and harmonizing effects.
- **Vanilla**: Invoking sensuality and comfort, vanilla is a powerful herb for nurturing the soul and fostering personal connections.

### Mars-Influenced Herbs

Mars rules energy, action, and desire. Herbs associated with Mars generally have stimulating effects, boost energy, and support muscle and blood health.

- **Garlic**: Known for its protective and invigorating properties, garlic boosts vitality and combats infections.
- **Nettle**: A tonic that supports blood health and energy, nettle embodies Mars's dynamic and protective qualities.

## Jupiter-Influenced Herbs

Jupiter is associated with growth, expansion, and wisdom. Jupiterian herbs promote liver health, aid digestion, and encourage spiritual growth.

- **Dandelion**: With its expansive properties, dandelion supports liver function and digestion, reflecting Jupiter's influence on growth and nurturing.
- **Sage**: Used for wisdom and protection, sage promotes mental expansion and spiritual well-being.

## Saturn-Influenced Herbs

Saturn governs structure, discipline, and longevity. Saturnian herbs are used for bone health, skin structure, and aging concerns.

- **Horsetail**: Rich in silica, horsetail helps in strengthening bones and rejuvenating the skin.
- **Comfrey**: Known for healing bones and wounds, comfrey embodies Saturn's principles of restoration and resilience.

## Uranus-Influenced Herbs

Uranus influences change, innovation, and independence. Herbs under its influence tend to affect the nervous system and promote mental flexibility.

- **Ginkgo**: Ginkgo enhances cerebral blood flow, supporting brain health and mental clarity, mirroring Uranus's association with innovation and breakthrough.

## Neptune-Influenced Herbs

Neptune rules dreams, intuition, and psychic receptivity. Neptune-influenced herbs help dissolve boundaries, enhance psychic abilities, and promote dream work.

- **Mugwort**: Traditionally used for lucid dreaming and psychic exploration, mugwort facilitates deep spiritual and subconscious exploration.

**Pluto-Influenced Herbs**

Pluto governs transformation, rebirth, and healing at deep levels. Pluto-influenced herbs are potent and often used for detoxification and rebirth.

- **Basil**: Known for its detoxifying properties, basil can help release old habits and foster new beginnings, aligning with Pluto's transformative energy.

This chapter provides a comprehensive look at how each planet's energy influences specific herbs, offering a celestial pharmacy that aligns with the physical, emotional, and spiritual aspects of our lives. By understanding these relationships, practitioners of AstroHerbology can more effectively harness the healing powers of the herbal world in conjunction with the cosmic energies that permeate our universe.

Check out my Virtual dispensary for all your hemp needs: https://shift.store/sg1fan23477/retail

**Chapter 3: Elemental Herbalism - Earth, Water, Air, Fire**

Elemental Herbalism forms a fundamental aspect of AstroHerbology, aligning the energies of the four classical elements—Earth, Water, Air, and Fire—with herbal practices. Each element corresponds to different bodily systems, emotional states, and spiritual energies, influencing the healing properties of herbs. In this chapter of "The Starry Guide to Herbal Harmony: Volume 1," we explore how these elemental categories help us to understand and utilize herbs more effectively in balancing our health and enhancing our lives.

## Earth Herbs: Foundations of Stability and Nourishment

Earth herbs are synonymous with grounding, stability, and nourishment. These herbs typically support the physical structure of the body, such as bones and muscles, aid in digestion, and are vital in treating chronic conditions by building and sustaining health over time.

- **Alfalfa**: Known as the "father of all foods," alfalfa is deeply nourishing, rich in minerals, and supports bone health.
- **Slippery Elm**: Its soothing mucilage aids in healing and coating the digestive tract, making it ideal for gastrointestinal health.
- **Turmeric**: A powerful anti-inflammatory, turmeric supports joint and overall health, grounding the body's inflammatory responses.

These earth herbs play a crucial role in long-term health maintenance, acting as foundational supports that stabilize and nurture the body.

## Water Herbs: Flowing with Healing and Emotion

Water herbs are associated with emotional healing, fluidity, and intuition. These herbs often have a calming effect, helping to soothe anxiety and stress, and are used to enhance emotional release and psychic awareness.

- **Lemon Balm**: Known for its gentle soothing effects, lemon balm reduces anxiety and eases the nervous system.
- **Willow Bark**: Traditionally used for pain relief, willow bark's properties are akin to flowing water, easing the currents of pain and inflammation.
- **Kava Kava**: Excellent for its sedative properties, this herb is used to calm the mind and encourage emotional fluidity.

Water herbs are essential for managing emotional wellness, promoting a healthy flow of emotions, and enhancing intuitive capabilities.

## Air Herbs: Enhancing Mind and Breath

Air herbs are linked with the cognitive and respiratory systems. They support communication, thought processes, and respiratory health, making them indispensable for those seeking mental clarity and improved airway function.

- **Ginkgo Biloba**: Renowned for its ability to enhance cognitive function and memory, Ginkgo promotes cerebral blood flow.
- **Mullein**: A classic herb for lung health, mullein helps to clear congestion and promote better breathing.
- **Peppermint**: With its invigorating scent, peppermint lifts the spirit and stimulates clear thinking, while also aiding digestion.

Air herbs are pivotal in treatments aiming to enhance mental agility and respiratory health, offering relief and support to these vital areas.

## Fire Herbs: Igniting Vitality and Passion

Fire herbs are energizing and warming, focusing on boosting metabolism, courage, and passion. These herbs are used to address conditions of lethargy, cold, and lack of motivation, igniting the internal flames of vitality and drive.

- **Ginger**: A warming herb that stimulates circulation and boosts metabolic rate, ginger is ideal for stoking the digestive fire.
- **Cayenne**: Known for its heat, cayenne enhances circulation, raises energy levels, and builds heat within the body.
- **Cinnamon**: Besides its warming properties, cinnamon sparks digestive fire and enhances blood sugar control, fueling the body's energetic needs.

Fire herbs are crucial for stimulating energy within the body, enhancing warmth and vitality, and reigniting the passion for life, especially in those who feel energetically depleted.

By understanding the elemental associations of these herbs, practitioners of AstroHerbology can more effectively address a wide range of physical, emotional, and spiritual needs. This holistic approach not only considers the symptoms that need alleviation but also aligns the treatment with the elemental nature of the individual, ensuring a balanced and harmonious healing process. This chapter serves as a guide to selecting the right herbs based on the elemental needs of each person, integrating ancient wisdom with practical healing.

Check out my Virtual dispensary for all your hemp needs: https://shift.store/sg1fan23477/retail

**Chapter 4: Harnessing the Moon's Power in Herbal Practice**

The moon, with its mystical and powerful presence, plays a vital role in AstroHerbology. Its influence permeates every aspect of herbal practice, from the planting of seeds to the crafting of potent elixirs. In "The Starry Guide to Herbal Harmony: Volume 1," this chapter explores how to align herbal activities with the lunar cycle, utilizing the moon's phases and astrological position to maximize the effectiveness of herbal remedies. Here, we delve into the practices of Moon Phase Gardening, Moon Sign Gardening, and the creation of Lunar Elixirs.

## Phases of the Moon and Planting Herbs

The lunar cycle, from new moon to full moon and back again, affects plant growth and potency. Each phase holds specific energies conducive to different herbal practices:

- **New Moon**: The new moon, signifying beginnings, is an ideal time to plant seeds. Herbs started during this phase are believed to absorb the growing energy of the waxing moon, leading to stronger, more resilient plants.
- **Waxing Moon**: As the moon grows fuller, it's an opportune time to nurture plants, encourage growth, and add nutrients to the soil.
- **Full Moon**: The full moon's energy is perfect for harvesting herbs, as their medicinal qualities are at their peak. The gravitational pull of the full moon causes more sap and essential oils to flow in the plant, enhancing their potency.
- **Waning Moon**: During the waning moon, it's time to clear away the old and prepare for the new. This phase is ideal for weeding, pruning, and harvesting roots and barks, which are best collected when the plant's energy is drawn downwards.

## Moon Sign Gardening

Beyond the phases, the moon's position in the zodiac also influences herbal work. Each zodiac sign imparts different qualities to plants:

- **Fire Signs (Aries, Leo, Sagittarius)**: Best for harvesting herbs that benefit from strong, fiery energy, like those used for increasing vitality and passion.
- **Earth Signs (Taurus, Virgo, Capricorn)**: Optimal for planting and transplanting. Earth signs contribute stability and growth to the roots.
- **Air Signs (Gemini, Libra, Aquarius)**: Favorable for flowers and aromatic herbs, these signs enhance the plant's scent and potency.
- **Water Signs (Cancer, Scorpio, Pisces)**: Ideal for planting and irrigation, as water signs help seeds germinate and young plants grow smoothly.

Timing your gardening activities by the moon sign can significantly influence the therapeutic qualities and growth efficiency of herbs.

## Creating Lunar Elixirs

Lunar elixirs harness the moon's energies, infusing herbal remedies with its potent vibrational qualities. Here's how to craft these powerful concoctions:

1. **Choosing Your Herbs**: Select herbs that correspond with the current lunar phase or sign for targeted healing properties. For example, chamomile during a full moon in Cancer for emotional soothing.
2. **Setting the Intention**: Before preparing your elixir, set a clear intention. What is the purpose of this elixir? Healing, protection, love? This will guide the energetic focus of your preparation.
3. **Crafting the Elixir**:
    - **Teas**: Infuse herbs in hot water under moonlight to create a lunar tea. The moon's energy will charge the water along with the herbs.
    - **Tinctures**: Soak herbs in alcohol with the jar exposed to moonlight for several nights to imbue it with lunar power.

- **Oils**: Place herbs and carrier oil in a clear container, letting it sit under the moon for one full cycle to draw in the energy.
4. **Storing and Using**: Store the elixirs in a cool, dark place. Use them as needed or during specific lunar phases to enhance their effects.

Through the practices detailed in this chapter, practitioners can deepen their connection to the lunar energies, significantly enhancing their herbal craft. By aligning planting, harvesting, and remedy creation with the moon's cycles and signs, herbalists can achieve a harmonious balance between celestial influence and earthly healing.

Check out my Virtual dispensary for all your hemp needs: https://shift.store/sg1fan23477/retail

**Chapter 5: The Herbal Zodiac - Signs, Plants, and Healing**

In AstroHerbology, the zodiac plays a crucial role in understanding how celestial energies influence botanical therapies. Each zodiac sign has unique characteristics, which correlate with specific health tendencies and herbal affinities. This chapter of "The Starry Guide to Herbal Harmony: Volume 1" explores the deep connection between the twelve zodiac signs and their corresponding herbs, offering tailored wellness rituals and herbal recipes to enhance well-being. The insights provided here aim to harmonize one's health with the rhythms of the cosmos.

## Aries (March 21 - April 19)

**Personality and Physical Correspondences:** Aries are known for their energetic, assertive nature. They often face challenges with head and facial areas like headaches, sinus issues, and acne.

**Sign-Specific Herbs:**

- **Ginger:** Energizes and stimulates, mirroring Aries' fiery energy.
- **Nettle:** Supports iron levels, boosting vitality and vigor.

**Wellness Rituals and Recipes:**

- **Energizing Tea:** A blend of ginger and nettle to invigorate the body and mind.
- **Facial Steam:** Using chamomile to reduce inflammation and clear sinus passages.

## Taurus (April 20 - May 20)

**Personality and Physical Correspondences:** Taurus individuals are grounded but can suffer from neck and throat ailments, including thyroid issues.

**Sign-Specific Herbs:**

- **Slippery Elm**: Soothes and protects the throat, enhancing vocal health.
- **Sage**: Supports overall throat health and digestion.

**Wellness Rituals and Recipes:**

- **Throat Soothing Syrup**: A concoction of slippery elm and honey.
- **Digestive Tea**: Blending sage and peppermint to promote digestive health.

## Gemini (May 21 - June 20)

**Personality and Physical Correspondences**: Geminis are communicative but may struggle with respiratory and nervous system issues.

**Sign-Specific Herbs:**

- **Lavender**: Calms the nerves and supports mental clarity.
- **Mullein**: Enhances lung function and respiratory health.

**Wellness Rituals and Recipes:**

- **Nerve-Soothing Tincture**: Lavender infused in a neutral spirit.
- **Respiratory Tea**: A combination of mullein and licorice root to aid breathing.

## Cancer (June 21 - July 22)

**Personality and Physical Correspondences**: Cancers are nurturing yet prone to digestive and emotional issues due to their sensitive nature.

**Sign-Specific Herbs:**

- **Chamomile**: Soothes both the digestive system and emotional upheavals.
- **Aloe Vera**: Heals and soothes stomach lining and skin.

**Wellness Rituals and Recipes:**

- **Soothing Gel Drink**: Aloe vera gel blended with a touch of honey.
- **Emotional Calm Tea**: Chamomile and lavender tea to ease emotional stress.

## Leo (July 23 - August 22)

**Personality and Physical Correspondences**: Leos have robust vitality but can face heart and back issues.

**Sign-Specific Herbs:**

- **Hawthorn**: Strengthens the heart and circulatory system.
- **Sunflower**: Represents the sun, boosting mood and energy.

**Wellness Rituals and Recipes:**

- **Heart Health Tincture**: Hawthorn berries soaked in alcohol.
- **Energizing Snack**: Sunflower seeds mixed with dried fruits.

## Virgo (August 23 - September 22)

**Personality and Physical Correspondences**: Virgos are meticulous but can suffer from digestive and nervous system complaints due to their often anxious nature.

**Sign-Specific Herbs:**

- **Peppermint**: Aids digestion and reduces stomach discomfort.
- **Valerian Root**: Relieves anxiety and promotes relaxation.

**Wellness Rituals and Recipes:**

- **Digestive Aid Capsules**: Ground peppermint leaves encapsulated for daily use.
- **Relaxation Tea**: Valerian root combined with chamomile for a soothing nighttime brew.

## Libra (September 23 - October 22)

**Personality and Physical Correspondences**: Libras are balanced but can have issues with kidneys and skin due to their focus on harmony and aesthetics.

**Sign-Specific Herbs:**

- **Cranberry**: Supports kidney health and urinary tract.
- **Rose**: Beautifies the skin and balances emotional health.

**Wellness Rituals and Recipes:**

- **Kidney Health Drink**: Pure cranberry juice diluted with water.
- **Balancing Facial Toner**: Rose water spritz for skin health and emotional balance.

## Scorpio (October 23 - November 21)

**Personality and Physical Correspondences**: Scorpios are intense with strong healing capabilities but may face reproductive and excretory system issues.

**Sign-Specific Herbs:**

- **Basil**: Detoxifies and stimulates healing.
- **Garlic**: Offers deep immune support and purifying effects.

**Wellness Rituals and Recipes:**

- **Purifying Broth**: A hearty broth infused with garlic and basil.
- **Immune Boosting Tincture**: Garlic macerated in alcohol to create a powerful immune supporter.

## Sagittarius (November 22 - December 21)

**Personality and Physical Correspondences**: Sagittarians are adventurous but may suffer from liver and hip issues.

**Sign-Specific Herbs:**

- **Milk Thistle**: Supports liver health and detoxification.
- **Turmeric**: Reduces inflammation and enhances mobility.

**Wellness Rituals and Recipes:**

- **Liver Detox Tea**: Milk thistle and dandelion root tea blend.
- **Anti-inflammatory Paste**: Turmeric paste for culinary use.

## Capricorn (December 22 - January 19)

**Personality and Physical Correspondences**: Capricorns are disciplined but can experience bone, teeth, and skin issues due to their structured nature.

**Sign-Specific Herbs:**

- **Horsetail**: Rich in silica, supports bone and skin health.
- **Comfrey**: Known for aiding in the healing of broken bones and bruises.

**Wellness Rituals and Recipes:**

- **Bone Strength Tea**: A decoction of horsetail for drinking.
- **Healing Salve**: Comfrey mixed with beeswax and oils for topical application.

## Aquarius (January 20 - February 18)

**Personality and Physical Correspondences**: Aquarians are innovative but may encounter issues with circulation and the ankles.

**Sign-Specific Herbs:**

- **Ginkgo Biloba**: Enhances circulation and cognitive function.
- **Yarrow**: Supports vascular health and internal healing.

**Wellness Rituals and Recipes:**

- **Circulatory Support Tincture**: Ginkgo leaves extracted in alcohol.
- **Healing Poultice**: Yarrow leaves crushed and applied to sprains or bruises.

## Pisces (February 19 - March 20)

**Personality and Physical Correspondences**: Pisces are empathetic but can have foot and lymphatic system issues, reflecting their fluid and intuitive nature.

**Sign-Specific Herbs:**

- **Elderflower**: Supports immune and respiratory health.
- **Lemon Balm**: Eases anxiety and helps with sleep.

**Wellness Rituals and Recipes:**

- **Respiratory Health Syrup**: Elderflower syrup for colds and flu.
- **Soothing Sleep Tea**: Lemon balm and lavender blend to promote restful sleep.

Each section of this chapter provides a comprehensive guide to understanding and using the zodiac's wisdom to select herbs that resonate with each sign's energy, enhancing personal health and spiritual growth. By integrating these insights into daily life, one can create a personalized approach to herbal wellness that aligns with the cosmic forces governing our lives.

Check out my Virtual dispensary for all your hemp needs: https://shift.store/sg1fan23477/retail

**Chapter 6: Planetary Days, Plants, and Potions**

AstroHerbology integrates celestial wisdom into the fabric of daily life, where each day of the week holds the energy of a specific planet. This ancient practice enhances the connection between daily activities and cosmic rhythms, offering a unique way to select herbs that harmonize with planetary energies. In this chapter of "The Starry Guide to Herbal Harmony: Volume 1," we explore how to harness the power of planetary days through specific herbs and rituals, providing a daily herbal routine and crafting recipes that align with each day's ruling planet.

## Working with Planetary Days

Each day of the week is traditionally associated with a celestial body, which influences various activities, including herbal practice:

- **Sunday (Sun)**: Vitality and success.
- **Monday (Moon)**: Healing and emotional work.
- **Tuesday (Mars)**: Energy and courage.
- **Wednesday (Mercury)**: Communication and intellect.
- **Thursday (Jupiter)**: Abundance and growth.
- **Friday (Venus)**: Love and beauty.
- **Saturday (Saturn)**: Cleansing and protection.

Understanding these associations allows herbalists to choose plants that resonate best with the day's planetary energy, enhancing their effectiveness.

## Daily Herbal Routines

Incorporating specific herbs into daily wellness practices can optimize health and harmony. Here's how to align your herbal routine with the planetary energies of each day:

- **Sunday**: Focus on heart health and vitality using herbs like **Sunflower** and **Calendula**. Start the day with a sunflower seed smoothie or a calendula-infused oil massage to invoke the Sun's vibrant energy.
- **Monday**: Use soothing herbs like **Chamomile** and **Moonwort** to enhance emotional well-being. A chamomile tea at bedtime or a moonwort compress can help start the week with a sense of calm.
- **Tuesday**: Harness the fiery energy of Mars with herbs like **Ginger** and **Nettle**. A morning tonic of ginger tea can stimulate energy, while adding nettle to your diet can boost courage and vitality.
- **Wednesday**: Enhance communication with Mercury-related herbs such as **Lavender** and **Eucalyptus**. Lavender-infused honey in your tea can aid clarity of thought, or use eucalyptus oil in a diffuser to clear the mind.
- **Thursday**: Jupiter's abundance can be tapped with herbs like **Sage** and **Dandelion**. A sage smudging ritual can clear negative energy, promoting growth and prosperity, while dandelion tea can support liver health and digestion.
- **Friday**: Venus's influence is perfect for beauty and love-enhancing herbs like **Rose** and **Vanilla**. A luxurious rose petal bath or a vanilla bean dessert can heighten beauty and attract love.
- **Saturday**: Use Saturn's grounding energy with detoxifying herbs like **Horsetail** and **Comfrey**. A horsetail hair rinse or a comfrey leaf poultice can help cleanse and protect the body at week's end.

## Planetary Herbal Recipes

Creating herbal recipes that correspond to the planetary energies of each day can deeply enhance the spiritual and physical benefits of herbs:

- **Sun Tea**: Blend calendula, sunflower petals, and cinnamon for a warm, invigorating start to your Sunday.
- **Moon Bath**: A soothing bath soak with moonwort, chamomile, and lavender to calm and restore on Monday.

- **Mars Incense**: Burn dried ginger and nettle with a pinch of cayenne to invigorate your space on Tuesday.
- **Mercury Elixir**: A tincture of lavender and peppermint to enhance communication and mental alertness for Wednesday.
- **Jupiter Poultice**: Apply a sage and dandelion leaf poultice to promote healing and prosperity on Thursday.
- **Venus Facial Mask**: A rose petal and vanilla bean mask for beauty treatments on Friday.
- **Saturn Cleansing Scrub**: Use ground horsetail and charcoal for a powerful detoxifying scrub on Saturday.

By integrating these practices into your weekly routine, you can align more closely with the planetary energies, enhancing your health, well-being, and spiritual growth. This chapter provides a structured yet flexible framework that invites both novice and experienced practitioners to explore and benefit from the rich tapestry of AstroHerbology. Each day offers a unique opportunity to deepen your connection with the universe through the wise and purposeful use of herbs.

Check out my Virtual dispensary for all your hemp needs: https://shift.store/sg1fan23477/retail

**Chapter 7: Astrological Herbal Formulations**

In the realm of AstroHerbology, the art of crafting personalized herbal remedies based on astrological insights stands as a profound method of healing. This chapter of "The Starry Guide to Herbal Harmony: Volume 1" delves into the nuances of creating bespoke herbal blends that not only address specific health concerns but also enhance overall vitality by aligning with cosmic rhythms. We explore the principles of astrological timing in herbal preparations and provide illustrative case studies that showcase the efficacy of this holistic approach.

## Crafting Personalized Herbal Remedies

Creating personalized herbal remedies requires an understanding of an individual's astrological chart, which offers insights into their inherent strengths, susceptibilities, and the root of potential health issues. Here's how to approach this:

1. **Analyze the Natal Chart**: Identify dominant planets and signs, particularly noting any planets in detriment or those that aspect the Ascendant or ruler of the sixth house of health.
2. **Identify Health Concerns**: Relate astrological insights to physical conditions. For instance, a heavily aspected Mars might indicate inflammatory conditions, while Saturn might point to chronic issues or coldness.
3. **Select Corresponding Herbs**: Choose herbs that resonate with the necessary planetary energy to balance the identified concerns. For example, use soothing, Moon-associated herbs like chamomile for emotional sensitivity or Mars-associated herbs like garlic for boosting immunity and energy.
4. **Formulate the Remedy**: Combine herbs in a form that the patient will consistently use, such as teas, tinctures, or topical applications.

The proportions can be influenced by the strength of planetary influences in the natal chart.

## Astrological Timing for Herbal Preparations

The timing of preparing herbal remedies is critical in AstroHerbology. Utilizing planetary hours, moon phases, and significant astrological events can greatly enhance the effectiveness of herbal preparations:

1. **Planetary Hours**: Each day is divided into planetary hours, which are periods that are ruled by a particular planet. Crafting a remedy during a specific planetary hour can enhance its properties (e.g., creating a Venusian love tonic during a Venus hour).
2. **Moon Phases**: The phase of the moon can impact the potency of herbal remedies. For example, concocting a growth-promoting herbal tonic during the waxing moon, or a detoxifying blend during the waning moon.
3. **Astrological Events**: Significant alignments such as eclipses, solstices, or planetary conjunctions can be potent times for preparing remedies aimed at major healings or transformations.

## Case Studies

### Case Study 1: Managing Migraines

- **Client**: A Gemini Ascendant with Mercury in the 6th house afflicted by Saturn.
- **Symptom**: Chronic migraines.
- **Herbal Remedy**: A blend of lavender (to soothe Mercury's nerves) and feverfew (to counteract Saturn's cold and restrictive influence), prepared during Mercury's hour on a Wednesday close to the New Moon (signifying new beginnings in health).
- **Outcome**: Reduction in migraine frequency and intensity after consistently using the remedy over three lunar cycles.

### Case Study 2: Enhancing Digestive Health

- **Client:** A Virgo Ascendant with Jupiter in detriment in the 6th house.
- **Symptom:** Digestive inefficiency and bloating.
- **Herbal Remedy:** A digestive aid tea made from peppermint (to soothe and stimulate digestion) and dandelion root (to support Jupiter and liver function), crafted during Jupiter's hour on a Thursday when the Moon was in Cancer (focusing on nurturing and stomach-related issues).
- **Outcome:** Improved digestion and less bloating within one month of daily use.

## Case Study 3: Emotional Well-being

- **Client:** A Cancer Ascendant with Moon in the 12th house opposed by Pluto.
- **Symptom:** Emotional distress and periodic depression.
- **Herbal Remedy:** An emotional balancer syrup using rose (to nurture Cancer's sensitivity and soothe the heart) and skullcap (to mitigate Pluto's intense emotional upheaval), prepared during the Full Moon to draw down maximum emotional healing power.
- **Outcome:** Enhanced emotional resilience and mood stabilization observed over several months.

These case studies illustrate the transformative potential of integrating astrological insights into herbal practice. By understanding the unique celestial blueprint of each individual, practitioners can tailor remedies that precisely target and amend health imbalances, ushering in a harmonized state of well-being that aligns with both the cosmos and the natural world.

Check out my Virtual dispensary for all your hemp needs: https://shift.store/sg1fan23477/retail

**Conclusion: A Cosmic Path to Herbal Harmony**

As we conclude "The Starry Guide to Herbal Harmony: Volume 1," it is evident that the journey into AstroHerbology is both enriching and profound. This ancient yet ever-relevant practice provides a unique lens through which we can view our health and wellness, connecting the microcosm of our individual existence with the macrocosm of the universe. Integrating AstroHerbology into daily life enriches routine activities with a layer of celestial significance, turning everyday actions into meaningful rituals.

## Integrating AstroHerbology into Everyday Life

**Gardening**: Align your gardening practices with the lunar cycle for more robust plant growth and potent herbal yields. Plant during the New Moon, harvest during the Full Moon, and consider the astrological sign the Moon is transiting to maximize the therapeutic qualities of your herbs.

**Cooking**: Incorporate herbs into your daily meals according to planetary days. For example, use Sun-associated herbs like rosemary on Sundays to invigorate and uplift your spirit or Moon-associated herbs like cucumbers on Mondays to promote emotional balance and hydration.

**Self-care Practices**: Create a self-care routine with herbal products aligned with your personal astrological chart. For instance, if Mars influences your health sector, using ginger baths or scrubs can boost your vitality and courage. Tailoring these practices to your astrological influences can enhance your physical and emotional well-being.

## Continuing the Journey

The path of AstroHerbology is endless and ever-evolving. Each step on this path deepens your connection with the natural world and the cosmos, revealing new insights and methods to enhance health and spiritual well-being. We encourage you to keep exploring this fascinating intersection between astrology and herbalism. Experiment with different herbs, track the lunar phases, and observe how the planets influence your health and energy levels. Your personal experiences will contribute to a deeper understanding and a richer practice.

## Resources for Further Exploration

To further your exploration of AstroHerbology, consider delving into the following resources:

**Books:**

- "The Complete Guide to Astrological Self-Care" by Stephanie Gailing offers a comprehensive look at using astrology to enhance wellness practices.
- "Planetary Herbology" by Michael Tierra links the ancient wisdom of the East and West, providing detailed information on the energetic properties of herbs through the lens of astrology.
- "Medical Astrology" by Judith Hill explores how astrological signs impact health, offering insights into herbal treatments tailored to astrological profiles.

**Websites:**

- Astro.com provides free astrological charts and insightful articles that help personalize your astrological understanding.
- The Mountain Astrologer (mountainastrologer.com) features articles on diverse astrological topics, including health and herbalism.
- HerbRally (herbrally.com) hosts a variety of podcasts and articles on herbal medicine practices and traditions.

**Courses:**

- The School of Evolutionary Herbalism offers courses on the synergy between plant medicine and astrological wisdom.
- Kepler College (kepler.edu) provides classes on medical astrology that can enhance your understanding of astrological influences on health.

By engaging with these resources, you can expand your knowledge and refine your practice in AstroHerbology. As you blend the rich traditions of astrology and herbalism, you create a harmonious lifestyle that not only nurtures your body but also aligns you with the rhythms of the cosmos. May your journey through the cosmic and herbal realms bring you closer to the harmony and balance that AstroHerbology promises. Embrace this path as you continue to explore and integrate the wisdom of the stars and the healing power of the Earth into your life.

## A. Glossary of Terms

In "The Starry Guide to Herbal Harmony: Volume 1," numerous terms and concepts are integral to understanding the connection between astrology and herbalism. This glossary serves as a resource for defining these key terms, ensuring clarity and depth of understanding for all readers, regardless of their prior knowledge or experience.

## Aspects

**Aspects** refer to the specific angles formed between planets in the sky, as viewed from Earth. These angles determine how the energies of the planets interact and influence events on Earth, including plant growth and herbal efficacy. Common aspects include conjunctions (0 degrees), sextiles (60 degrees), squares (90 degrees), trines (120 degrees), and oppositions (180 degrees).

## Decoction

A **Decoction** is a method of herbal extraction that involves boiling plant material in water. The boiling process breaks down the plant's cell walls, releasing soluble chemicals into the water. This method is particularly effective for extracting the active ingredients from tougher plant materials like roots, barks, and dense leaves.

## Ecliptic

The **Ecliptic** is the apparent path that the Sun follows through the sky over the course of the year as a result of Earth's orbit around the Sun. In astrology, the ecliptic is used to define the positions of the zodiac signs through which the Sun appears to move as the Earth orbits.

## Zodiac Signs

**Zodiac Signs** are the twelve 30-degree sectors of the ecliptic, each representing a different segment of the sky. The signs—Aries, Taurus, Gemini, Cancer, Leo, Virgo, Libra, Scorpio, Sagittarius, Capricorn, Aquarius, and Pisces—play a critical role in astrology by influencing various energies and traits.

## Planetary Rulerships

**Planetary Rulerships** refer to the association between planets and the signs they govern. Each zodiac sign is ruled by a planet that significantly influences its expression. For example, Mars rules Aries, imparting qualities of assertiveness and initiative.

## Natal Chart

A **Natal Chart** is a map of where all the planets were in their journey around the Sun, from our viewpoint on earth, at the exact moment of a person's birth. This chart is used in astrology to interpret character traits, life events, and health tendencies.

## Herbal Tinctures

**Herbal Tinctures** are concentrated herbal extracts made by soaking herbs in alcohol or vinegar. The solvent pulls out the active compounds from the herbs, creating a potent liquid that preserves the medicinal properties for extended periods.

## Infusion

An **Infusion** is a gentle method of extracting herbal compounds by steeping herbs in hot water. This method is typically used for delicate parts of the plant, such as leaves and flowers, which release their active ingredients at lower temperatures.

## Planetary Hours

**Planetary Hours** are segments of time during the day or night that are ruled by a particular planet, each influencing certain activities. These hours are calculated based on the time of sunrise and sunset, and they cycle through the seven traditional planets (Sun, Moon, Mars, Mercury, Jupiter, Venus, Saturn) in a specific order.

## Elemental Properties

**Elemental Properties** refer to the association of herbs with the four classical elements: earth, water, air, and fire. Each element corresponds to different characteristics and healing properties of herbs, influencing how they are used in treatment.

## Moon Phases

**Moon Phases** describe the changing appearance of the Moon as it orbits Earth, directly influencing herbal potency when harvesting or planting. The main phases are new moon, waxing crescent, first quarter, waxing gibbous, full moon, waning gibbous, last quarter, and waning crescent.

This glossary provides the foundational vocabulary necessary to fully appreciate and utilize the teachings of "The Starry Guide to Herbal Harmony: Volume 1." By understanding these terms, readers can more effectively connect the celestial influences with the earthly practice of herbalism, enhancing both their knowledge and their practical skills in natural healing.

## B. Astrological Symbol Chart

In "The Starry Guide to Herbal Harmony: Volume 1," an understanding of astrological symbols enhances the connection between celestial phenomena and herbal practices. This section provides a detailed chart of astrological symbols commonly used in astrology, including those for the signs of the zodiac, planets, and significant aspects. This chart serves as a quick reference to help readers visually identify and familiarize themselves with these essential symbols, which are often encountered in astrological charts and literature.

## Zodiac Signs

The zodiac signs and their symbols are foundational in astrology, representing different segments of the ecliptic through which the planets move:

1. **Aries** (♈) - The Ram: Represents initiation, courage, and pioneering.
2. **Taurus** (♉) - The Bull: Embodies stability, practicality, and sensuality.
3. **Gemini** (♊) - The Twins: Signifies communication, duality, and curiosity.
4. **Cancer** (♋) - The Crab: Associated with emotions, home, and nurturing.
5. **Leo** (♌) - The Lion: Expresses creativity, pride, and generosity.
6. **Virgo** (♍) - The Virgin: Symbolizes meticulousness, service, and practicality.
7. **Libra** (♎) - The Scales: Represents balance, harmony, and fairness.
8. **Scorpio** (♏) - The Scorpion: Conveys depth, transformation, and intensity.
9. **Sagittarius** (♐) - The Archer: Indicates exploration, philosophy, and freedom.

10. **Capricorn (♑)** - The Goat: Denotes discipline, ambition, and caution.
11. **Aquarius (♒)** - The Water Bearer: Reflects innovation, uniqueness, and humanitarianism.
12. **Pisces (♓)** - The Fishes: Embodies intuition, spirituality, and compassion.

## Planets

Each planet in astrology is associated with specific attributes and influences:

- **Sun (☉)**: Vitality, self, and power.
- **Moon ( ☽)**: Emotions, instincts, and habits.
- **Mercury (☿)**: Communication, intellect, and flexibility.
- **Venus (♀)**: Love, beauty, and harmony.
- **Mars (♂)**: Action, desire, and aggression.
- **Jupiter (♃)**: Growth, optimism, and abundance.
- **Saturn (♄)**: Structure, responsibility, and discipline.
- **Uranus (♅)**: Change, innovation, and rebellion.
- **Neptune (♆)**: Dreams, illusions, and intuition.
- **Pluto (♇)**: Transformation, power, and renewal.

## Aspects

Aspects describe the angles between planets, influencing how their energies combine:

- **Conjunction (☌)**: Planets at the same degree, amplifying each other's influence.
- **Sextile (⚹)**: Planets 60 degrees apart, enabling harmony and stimulation.
- **Square (□)**: Planets 90 degrees apart, indicating challenge and conflict.
- **Trine (△)**: Planets 120 degrees apart, promoting ease and flow.

- **Opposition (☍)**: Planets 180 degrees apart, reflecting balance or tension.

## Chart Representation

Ideally, this appendix would include a visual chart with each symbol clearly illustrated and labeled. This visual representation allows for quick identification and assists in making connections between the astrological configurations discussed in the text and the practical herbal applications. Readers can refer back to this chart whenever they encounter a symbol in the book, facilitating a deeper understanding and more intuitive learning experience.

By incorporating this astrological symbol chart in "The Starry Guide to Herbal Harmony: Volume 1," we provide readers with a valuable tool that enriches their exploration of AstroHerbology, bridging the celestial and the terrestrial in their quest for holistic health and cosmic alignment.

**C. Herbal Profiles**

In "The Starry Guide to Herbal Harmony: Volume 1," each herb discussed is paired with specific astrological insights to enhance its therapeutic potential. This section, Herbal Profiles, provides detailed information on each herb, including its botanical name, common uses, astrological associations, and important safety notes. This comprehensive approach ensures that readers can confidently integrate these herbs into their AstroHerbology practices.

## 1. Ginger (Zingiber officinale)

- **Common Uses**: Ginger is widely used for its anti-inflammatory properties, effectiveness in alleviating nausea, and its role in boosting digestion and circulation.
- **Astrological Associations**: Associated with Mars due to its spicy and warming nature, ginger is used to energize and stimulate action.
- **Safety Notes**: Ginger should be used cautiously by those with gallstones, and those on blood thinners should consult a healthcare provider due to its blood-thinning properties.

## 2. Lavender (Lavandula angustifolia)

- **Common Uses**: Lavender is renowned for its calming and relaxing effects, often used to alleviate stress, improve sleep, and soothe skin irritations.
- **Astrological Associations**: Ruled by Mercury, lavender supports communication and calmness, aiding in relaxation and mental clarity.
- **Safety Notes**: Generally safe for most people, though some may experience allergic reactions. Lavender oil should be diluted before topical application.

## 3. Chamomile (Matricaria recutita)

- **Common Uses**: Chamomile is primarily used for its soothing effects on the digestive system and for its ability to relieve insomnia and anxiety.
- **Astrological Associations**: Associated with the Sun and Moon, reflecting its ability to heal and soothe both physically and emotionally.
- **Safety Notes**: Chamomile should be avoided by those allergic to other plants in the daisy family. It may interact with blood thinners and sedative medications.

## 4. Nettle (Urtica dioica)

- **Common Uses**: Nettle is used for its rich mineral content, ability to relieve allergic symptoms, and as a support for joint health.
- **Astrological Associations**: Mars governs nettle, highlighting its ability to energize and support the blood and circulation.
- **Safety Notes**: Fresh nettle can cause skin irritation upon contact, though cooked or dried nettle is safe for most people. It should be used with caution in people with kidney issues.

## 5. Hawthorn (Crataegus spp.)

- **Common Uses**: Hawthorn is extensively used to support cardiovascular health, enhance blood flow, and maintain blood pressure.
- **Astrological Associations**: Ruled by Venus, hawthorn is beneficial in nurturing the heart, both physically and emotionally.
- **Safety Notes**: Hawthorn should be used under supervision when combined with prescription heart medications, as it can potentiate their effects.

## 6. Rose (Rosa spp.)

- **Common Uses**: Rose is used for its anti-inflammatory and astringent properties, benefiting skin health, emotional well-being, and digestion.

- **Astrological Associations**: Venus rules rose, emphasizing its harmonizing and beautifying effects.
- **Safety Notes**: Generally safe, but some individuals may experience allergic reactions, especially with topical use of rose oil.

## 7. Milk Thistle (Silybum marianum)

- **Common Uses**: Milk thistle is primarily known for its liver-protective effects, used to detoxify and regenerate liver tissue.
- **Astrological Associations**: Associated with Jupiter, which reflects its protective and growth-promoting properties.
- **Safety Notes**: Milk thistle is generally safe but may interact with certain medications affecting liver enzymes. Always check with a healthcare provider.

## 8. Eucalyptus (Eucalyptus globulus)

- **Common Uses**: Eucalyptus is used for respiratory health, clearing congestion, and as an antimicrobial agent.
- **Astrological Associations**: Ruled by the Moon, which enhances its cooling and soothing properties.
- **Safety Notes**: Eucalyptus oil should be used externally and never taken internally. It must be diluted for topical use and avoided around the face or nose of children.

This herbal profile section equips readers with essential knowledge about the therapeutic and astrological attributes of each herb, alongside crucial safety considerations. By providing this detailed information, "The Starry Guide to Herbal Harmony: Volume 1" ensures that readers can practice AstroHerbology safely and effectively, integrating these powerful natural remedies into their health regimens with precision and care.

### D. Moon Phase Calendar

The Moon Phase Calendar is an essential tool for practitioners of AstroHerbology, as it allows for precise planning of gardening, harvesting, and remedy preparation activities aligned with lunar energies. Understanding the phases of the moon and their influence on plant growth and herbal potency can significantly enhance the effectiveness of herbal practices. This section of "The Starry Guide to Herbal Harmony: Volume 1" provides a detailed calendar of the moon phases for the current year, helping readers synchronize their herbal activities with the rhythms of the moon.

## Key to Moon Phases

- **New Moon**: Ideal for setting intentions, starting new projects, and planting seeds.
- **Waxing Crescent**: Focus on growth, nourishment, and care for emerging plants.
- **First Quarter**: Good for building momentum, tackling challenges, and encouraging growth.
- **Waxing Gibbous**: Prepare for maturity, increase efforts in gardening, and focus on the health of plants.
- **Full Moon**: Peak energy for harvesting herbs, as their potency is at its maximum. Also, a powerful time for preparing potent herbal remedies.
- **Waning Gibbous**: Begin the process of culling, pruning, and harvesting where necessary.
- **Last Quarter**: Focus on maintenance, transplanting, and preparation for the next cycle.
- **Waning Crescent**: Rest, reflect, and plan. A time to conserve energy and clear out the old.

## Moon Phase Calendar for 2024

**January**

- New Moon: Jan 11
- First Quarter: Jan 18
- Full Moon: Jan 25
- Last Quarter: Jan 31

## February

- New Moon: Feb 10
- First Quarter: Feb 17
- Full Moon: Feb 24
- Last Quarter: Feb 28

## March

- New Moon: Mar 11
- First Quarter: Mar 18
- Full Moon: Mar 25
- Last Quarter: Mar 31

## April

- New Moon: Apr 9
- First Quarter: Apr 16
- Full Moon: Apr 23
- Last Quarter: Apr 30

## May

- New Moon: May 9
- First Quarter: May 15
- Full Moon: May 22
- Last Quarter: May 29

## June

- New Moon: Jun 7
- First Quarter: Jun 14
- Full Moon: Jun 21
- Last Quarter: Jun 28

## July

- New Moon: Jul 7
- First Quarter: Jul 13
- Full Moon: Jul 20
- Last Quarter: Jul 27

## August

- New Moon: Aug 5
- First Quarter: Aug 12
- Full Moon: Aug 19
- Last Quarter: Aug 27

## September

- New Moon: Sep 4
- First Quarter: Sep 10
- Full Moon: Sep 17
- Last Quarter: Sep 25

## October

- New Moon: Oct 3
- First Quarter: Oct 10
- Full Moon: Oct 17
- Last Quarter: Oct 25

## November

- New Moon: Nov 2
- First Quarter: Nov 9
- Full Moon: Nov 15
- Last Quarter: Nov 23

## December

- New Moon: Dec 1
- First Quarter: Dec 9
- Full Moon: Dec 15
- Last Quarter: Dec 22

This calendar provides a visual guide to help you align your herbal activities with the phases of the moon throughout the year. By planning your planting, nurturing, harvesting, and remedy-making activities according to these phases, you can optimize the effectiveness of your herbal practices and deepen your connection with the natural world.

### E. Planetary Hours Table

In AstroHerbology, understanding and utilizing planetary hours can greatly enhance the effectiveness of herbal activities, from planting and harvesting to crafting potent remedies. Planetary hours are periods during the day and night that are governed by specific planets, each influencing certain activities according to its astrological properties. This section of "The Starry Guide to Herbal Harmony: Volume 1" provides a detailed guide on how to calculate planetary hours for any given day, allowing practitioners to align their herbal practices with the optimal celestial energies.

## Understanding Planetary Hours

Planetary hours are based on the ancient Chaldean order of the planets, which is arranged according to their apparent speed as observed from Earth. The order from slowest to fastest is: Saturn, Jupiter, Mars, Sun, Venus, Mercury, and Moon. This sequence influences various aspects of life according to the characteristics associated with each planet.

## How to Calculate Planetary Hours

1. **Determine Sunrise and Sunset Times**: The first step in calculating planetary hours is to find out the exact times of sunrise and sunset for your location on the specific day you are interested in. This information can usually be found in local weather reports or online almanacs.

2. **Calculate Daylight Hours**: Subtract the time of sunrise from the time of sunset to find out the total duration of daylight. For

example, if sunrise is at 6:00 AM and sunset is at 6:00 PM, the total daylight time is 12 hours.

3. **Divide Daylight into Planetary Hours**: Divide the total daylight duration by 12 to find the duration of each planetary hour during the day. Using the example above, each planetary hour would be one hour long.

4. **Assign Planetary Rulers to Each Hour**: Start with the planetary ruler of the day at sunrise and follow the Chaldean order. For example, on Sunday, the Sun rules the first hour, followed by Venus, Mercury, Moon, Saturn, Jupiter, Mars, repeating the sequence until sunset.

5. **Calculate Nighttime Hours**: Apply the same method to the night hours, starting from sunset to the next day's sunrise. Divide the duration of the night by 12 and assign the planets in the same Chaldean order starting with the planet that follows the last planet of the daytime hours.

## Example of a Planetary Hours Table for a Specific Day

Assuming sunrise at 6:00 AM and sunset at 6:00 PM:

| Hour | Time | Planet |
| --- | --- | --- |
| 1st Hour | 6:00 - 7:00 AM | Sun |
| 2nd Hour | 7:00 - 8:00 AM | Venus |
| 3rd Hour | 8:00 - 9:00 AM | Mercury |
| 4th Hour | 9:00 - 10:00 AM | Moon |
| 5th Hour | 10:00 - 11:00 AM | Saturn |
| 6th Hour | 11:00 - 12:00 PM | Jupiter |
| 7th Hour | 12:00 - 1:00 PM | Mars |
| 8th Hour | 1:00 - 2:00 PM | Sun |

| 9th Hour | 2:00 - 3:00 PM | Venus |
| 10th Hour | 3:00 - 4:00 PM | Mercury |
| 11th Hour | 4:00 - 5:00 PM | Moon |
| 12th Hour | 5:00 - 6:00 PM | Saturn |

The same sequence applies for the night hours starting from 6:00 PM with Jupiter as the next planet.

## Utilizing Planetary Hours in Herbal Practice

By selecting specific times to perform herbal tasks according to the ruling planet, practitioners can enhance the desired effects of their activities. For example, harvesting warrior herbs like garlic during Mars hours can boost their potency, or crafting love potions during Venus hours can enhance their effectiveness.

This table and the methodology provided in "The Starry Guide to Herbal Harmony: Volume 1" empower practitioners to harness planetary energies, deepening the resonance between their herbal work and the astrological influences that govern these practices.

## F. Recipes and Remedies

In "The Starry Guide to Herbal Harmony: Volume 1," we emphasize the integration of herbal practices with astrological insights to foster health and well-being. This section offers additional recipes and remedies that combine the potent properties of herbs with specific celestial energies. These preparations are designed to be versatile, allowing practitioners to customize them based on their individual needs and the specific astrological conditions of any given time.

## 1. Solar Vitality Tonic

**Purpose**: To boost energy and strengthen the immune system.

- **Ingredients**:
    - 1 part ginger root (freshly grated)
    - 1 part lemon peel
    - 1/2 part turmeric root (freshly grated)
    - Honey to taste
    - Water
- **Astrological Association**: Sun (ideal to prepare on a Sunday for enhanced vitality)
- **Instructions**:
    - Combine ginger, lemon peel, and turmeric in a saucepan with about 2 cups of water.
    - Bring to a boil, then simmer for 10-15 minutes.
    - Strain the mixture and add honey while still warm.
    - Drink warm or cool. Consume daily in the morning to invigorate your day.

## 2. Lunar Calming Mist

**Purpose**: To promote relaxation and enhance sleep quality.

- **Ingredients**:

- ◦ 1 part lavender flowers
- ◦ 1 part chamomile flowers
- ◦ Witch hazel or distilled water
- ◦ Essential oil of lavender (optional)
- **Astrological Association**: Moon (best prepared on a Monday to harness soothing lunar energies)
- **Instructions**:
  - ◦ Infuse lavender and chamomile in witch hazel or distilled water by placing the herbs in a jar, covering them with the liquid, and letting sit for a full lunar cycle.
  - ◦ Strain the herbs and transfer the liquid to a spray bottle.
  - ◦ Add a few drops of lavender essential oil for added aromatherapeutic benefits.
  - ◦ Use as a room spray or linen mist before bedtime to induce tranquility and sleep.

## 3. Mercury Communication Tea

**Purpose**: To aid in clear communication and mental alertness.

- **Ingredients**:
  - ◦ 1 part peppermint leaf
  - ◦ 1/2 part rosemary leaf
  - ◦ 1/2 part lemon balm
- **Astrological Association**: Mercury (prepare on a Wednesday to enhance the communicative properties)
- **Instructions**:
  - ◦ Mix all dried herbs together.
  - ◦ Use one teaspoon of the blend per cup of hot water.
  - ◦ Steep for 5-10 minutes, strain, and drink.
  - ◦ Consume before important discussions or during study sessions to improve concentration and eloquence.

## 4. Venus Love Bath

**Purpose**: To attract love and foster personal beauty and harmony.

- **Ingredients:**
  - Rose petals
  - Jasmine flowers
  - Lavender buds
  - 1/4 cup Epsom salt
- **Astrological Association**: Venus (best prepared on a Friday to draw in Venusian influences)
- **Instructions:**
  - Combine all floral ingredients with Epsom salt in a large bowl.
  - Draw a warm bath and add the herbal mixture.
  - Soak in the bath while meditating on your desires related to love and personal satisfaction.

## 5. Saturn Stability Salve

**Purpose**: To aid in grounding and protect against negative energies.

- **Ingredients:**
  - 1 part comfrey leaf
  - 1 part plantain leaf
  - 1 part beeswax
  - Carrier oil (such as olive oil or coconut oil)
- **Astrological Association**: Saturn (prepare on a Saturday to enhance protective and grounding energies)
- **Instructions:**
  - Infuse comfrey and plantain in the carrier oil over low heat for 3 hours. Strain the herbs from the oil.
  - Add beeswax to the infused oil and heat until melted.
  - Pour the mixture into small tins or jars and allow to set.
  - Apply to the skin at pulse points or on the feet to promote grounding and stability.

These additional recipes and remedies provide readers with practical ways to incorporate AstroHerbology into their daily lives, enhancing personal health and spiritual well-being through the aligned energies of the cosmos and the healing power of herbs.

<u>Message from the Author:</u>

I hope you enjoyed this book, I love astrology and knew there was not a book such as this out on the shelf. I love metaphysical items as well. Please check out my other books:

-Life of Government Benefits

-My life of Hell

-My life with Hydrocephalus

-Red Sky

-World Domination:Woman's rule

-World Domination:Woman's Rule 2: The War

-Life and Banishment of Apophis: book 1

-The Kidney Friendly Diet

-The Ultimate Hemp Cookbook

-Creating a Dispensary(legally)

-Cleanliness throughout life: the importance of showering from childhood to adulthood.

-Strong Roots: The Risks of Overcoddling children

-Hemp Horoscopes: Cosmic Insights and Earthly Healing

- Celestial Hemp Navigating the Zodiac: Through the Green Cosmos

-Astrological Hemp: Aligning The Stars with Earth's Ancient Herb

-The Astrological Guide to Hemp: Stars, Signs, and Sacred Leaves

-Green Growth: Innovative Marketing Strategies for your Hemp Products and Dispensary

-Cosmic Cannabis

-Astrological Munchies

-Henry The Hemp

-Zodiacal Roots: The Astrological Soul Of Hemp

**- Green Constellations: Intersection of Hemp and Zodiac**

-Hemp in The Houses: An astrological Adventure Through The Cannabis Galaxy

-Galactic Ganja Guide

Heavenly Hemp

Zodiac Leaves

Doctor Who Astrology

Cannastrology

Stellar Satvias and Cosmic Indicas

<u>Celestial Cannabis: A Zodiac Journey</u>

AstroHerbology: The Sky and The Soil: Volume 1

AstroHerbology:Celestial Cannabis:Volume 2

Cosmic Cannabis Cultivation

Check out my Virtual dispensary for all your hemp needs: https://shift.store/sg1fan23477/retail

If you want solar for your home go here: https://www.harborsolar.live/apophisenterprises/

**<u>Instagrams: @apophis_enterprises, @hempkingdom2024,</u>**

**@apophisbookemporium,**

**@apophisfashion,**

**@apophisscardshop**

**Twitter: @apophisenterpr1, Tiktok:@apophisenterprise**

**Youtube: @sg1fan23477**

**Podcast: Apophis Chat Zone:** https://open.spotify.com/show/5zXbrCLEV2xzCp8ybrfHsk?si=fb4d4fdbdce44dec

**Newsletter:** https://apophiss-newsletter-27c897.beehiiv.com/

Please use the last few pages of this book to take notes or be your journal.

Journal: